The
Lemonade
Legacy

PASSING MONEY LESSONS
TO THE NEXT GENERATION

Colin Evans

Evans Financial Group
SHREVEPORT, LOUISIANA

Colin Evans/Evans Financial Group
7600 Fern Ave.
Building 1200
Shreveport LA 71105
www.evansfinancialgroup.com

Book layout ©2013 BookDesignTemplates.com

Dependents to Independence/ Colin Evans. —1st ed.
ISBN 978-1086373622

Contents

Foreword by David Evans...i

Introduction v

Being a Role Model 1

Doing the Right Thing... 15

Adapting to Change.. 21

Working Hard.. 27

Reaching Goals 35

Divvying up the Money 41

Understanding Credit.. 59

Making Investments 67

Getting Professional Advice 75

About the Author 81

Contact.. 83

This book is dedicated to three people: my father and mother who raised and trained me, and to my little girl in whom I hope to fulfill and instill the same values, emotions, and spirit of being financially free.

A special thanks to Phillip Hatfield; if it weren't for that one breakfast meeting, this book might have never happened.

Your kids will be a reflection of how you behave. Show them how to succeed, don't just tell them.

—DAVE RAMSEY

Foreword
by David Evans

When my wife, Gale, and I grew up, we weren't really poor. But sometimes we could see poor from where we were. We always had food on the table and clothes on our back. Neither of us came from money. Gale and I worked every summer through high school to buy the things we wanted to have or to wear.

When I was ready to go away to college, my parents had about $500 to apply toward the cost. The rest was accomplished through working, saving, and of course, student loans. We weren't given a car in high school or college because our parents just weren't in a position to do so. We did not begrudge them, we just learned something called "work ethic" very early in life, and for that we are most thankful.

Gale and I got married when we were twenty and I had just completed my sophomore year at Lamar University in Beaumont, Texas. We had saved enough to buy a car for $550, largely due to Gale's saving habits. It was a 1963 Pontiac Catalina with mag wheels—really cool! Our honeymoon was spent driving from New Jersey to Florida to see relatives. From there we drove to Beaumont, Texas, to start a new life.

Once in Beaumont, we got a furnished apartment. Gale went to work full-time as a secretary and I worked part-time at the local newspaper. Our grocery budget was $15 a week. Yes, that stretched a lot more a long time ago, but we still had a budget. We received monetary gifts for our wedding and that was our stash, or nest egg. Other than using it for driving home after college was over, I don't think we ever tapped into that fund.

In 1972, I started a career in the life insurance business, which, over a period of time, evolved into owning a financial planning firm. Gale started as legal secretary and did that until 1977, when our son, Colin, was born.

Perhaps because of the business I was in, we closely watched how we spent our money. One of the first presentations we were taught in the insurance business was "pay yourself first." We still preach that, except we give back to the Lord by tithing first. Then we spend on ourselves.

Over the years our income grew, as did our savings and generosity to others (not just the church). We had and still have a nice lifestyle. It has been our plan all along to pass on to Colin our saving and giving habits. Based on what I have witnessed so far in his life, this book, and his example, the plan has worked.

I believe we teach our children not by who we say we are, but rather how they "see" we are. I have heard and have told others: "When God measures a man, He doesn't put the tape around his head or his wallet . . . He puts it around his heart."

When Colin and his daughter Emmi—my granddaughter—started the idea about the lemonade stand, I thought it was pretty neat. I knew from this endeavor that we had an impact on Colin and it would be instilled in our grandchild as well. Candidly, Emmi does not have to work to buy her own stuff, but the message of work ethic, tithing, and saving will hopefully remain with her for many years to come. Perhaps it could even be passed on to her children. Perhaps Evans Financial Group will be a three-generational firm.

I can say with reasonable accuracy that not all people in the financial services industry follow their own advice. I find this to be a moral, ethical, and certainly a financial dilemma. I am not sure how we can give financial advice to others if our own financial castle is crumbling.

While this chapter is penned by me, the values in this book are Colin's. The values he speaks of are also in the hearts of both myself and my wife: Colin's parents. I can personally attest that even though I was the one in the financial business, Gale's attitude on saving, paying bills on time, giving, etc., have been foundational in our marriage of fifty years as of August 23, 2019.

I gave a seminar several years ago and was sitting at a table with some of the attendees. One lady brought up the subject of loaning your children money. She explained she heard someone say once, "When you loan money to your kids, sometimes they pay you back."

I looked at the guest and said, "Do you know how much money my son owes me?" Colin was within earshot, so he perked up and said, "I want to hear this answer!" My answer to her was "Nothing ... because he hasn't borrowed any."

Our belief system and financial philosophy in not infallible, but it worked from us to Colin, and now from Colin to Emmi. I sincerely hope, as you read this book and share these ideas and philosophies with your children or grandchildren, that their life will be a blessing to you as well as the lives they touch.

Dave Evans,
President, Evans Financial Group

Introduction

Growing up as a kid with a father in the financial services industry was both a blessing and a curse.

It was a blessing because my parents raised me to understand the principles of saving money and helping those less fortunate. They taught me this based on their experiences, my father's career, and their faith.

It was a curse in the sense that I held my parents in such high regard and wanted to follow their example. So as I grew I thirsted to become the good and godly father that my dad has been all my life. He set a high standard, and I knew I wanted and needed to be the kind of man he is in my life.

The idea for this book has its beginnings in a lunch with one of my former bosses from my high school and college days. During the lunch, I shared a story of an exercise I had done with my little girl because I want to carry on the values, examples, and principles my father shared with me, to help guide her to have a life of prosperity and an entrepreneurial mindset.

I wondered about sharing those concepts in a broader way, for those who weren't fortunate to grow up with a father in the financial services industry, or parents who didn't always set good financial examples. Maybe as a parent or a grandparent, you also wonder how you can impact and affect the financial education and literacy of your child or grandchild. Maybe you need some guidance on how to be a role model and share your experiences.

That's what this book is about. I want this to be a sort of guide-book for you to use or to inspire conversations with younger generations. It's also a way for me to pass on the blessings of being the son of financially savvy parents.

This is for you: David and Gale Evans and Emerson "Emmi" Evans.

Colin Evans

CHAPTER ONE

Being a Role Model

As kids, we never fully understand the impact, the strains, or the struggles involving money matters. Heck, even as adults, it can be difficult at times to comprehend the full extent of our financial decisions.

I was blessed to grow up in a great neighborhood (which, it still is to this day) in a nice house: four bedrooms, three bathrooms, and about 2,400 square feet. It was nothing over-the-top magnificent, but there was no proof of any sort of struggle or poverty. I was blessed to have two parents who had a great deal of common sense, a good moral compass, and excellent financial acumen. They taught me to share my blessings with others, by tithing at church, for example.

I also feel we are sharing our blessings through our work as financial advisors, helping others learn to manage their options and accumulate wealth. With this book, we hope to pass forward those blessings even more, onto younger generations who we hope will be responsible, financially savvy investors and consumers.

In school, we learn how to read and write. We learn how to do science experiments and to recite the capitols of each of the fifty states. We learn how to do addition, subtraction, multiplication, and division. But most kids don't ever take a class in economics or personal finance. Did you?

Money and economics can sound like hard subjects to grasp, but with the current marketplace, the stressors in our lives and the stressors in the economy, it's important for everyone—even kids—to know. Whether we realize it or not, we're involved in economics every day. The thing is, a lot of people don't realize that. They (especially the younger generations) think the Federal Reserve or Wall Street issues that make headlines are so far removed from their lives that things couldn't possibly affect them. They may not see how things happening on a grand scale can drastically change their community or their personal lives.

I want to emphasize that people *can* live a better quality of life, but it depends on financial savvy and planning. I'm not saying everyone should have an economics degree, but you do need to see how your financial habits fit into the grander scheme of things. And it's not just your own financial habits, it's those of your following generations, your legacy, if you will, that have an effect.

We deal with economics in the career choices we make, the products we buy, the products we invest in. We deal with it when we choose where to live. Who doesn't want a good place to raise a family with reasonable property taxes, nearby amenities, and low crime rates? We deal with it when we choose where we'll eat or where we'll vacation. We deal with finance when we decide when and where we'll retire.

Those choices make ripples and they affect so many sectors of an economy: the service sector is involved when we choose to eat out, the health care sector is affected by which doctors we choose, the manufacturing sector by which products we buy.

I'm sure you tell your kids there are consequences to their decisions. If they decide to not do their homework, there will be repercussions. If they decide to lie or decide to take an item without paying for it, you make it clear there will be a resulting action, right? Well, of course you do. You want to raise good kids.

But are you raising good kids when it comes to making decisions about money? You want them to make good choices there, too.

Only seventeen states require high school students to take a course in personal finance, and most states fail at producing financially literate high school students.[1]

Is it any wonder, then, that living paycheck-to-paycheck is a way of life for most U.S. workers? Or that one in four workers don't set aside any savings each month? And that nearly three of every four workers say they are in debt today, and more than half think they always will be?[2] Those are very scary statistics, and you likely don't want your kid or grandkids among those numbers. That's not the kind of legacy you want to leave, is it?

If we expect kids to learn about money matters, earning potential, interest, investments, and much more, how or where should they learn those things? Maybe they can learn from you! Through your example, through your activities, through ways they can relate and see how important—and even fun—it can be to earn, save, and invest money.

---

[1] Nova, Annie. CNBC. February 8, 2018. "Financial education stalls, threatening kids' future economic health."
https://www.cnbc.com/2018/02/08/financial-education-stalls-threatening-kids-future-economic-health.html
[2] CareerBuilder. PRNewswire. August 24, 2017. "Living Paycheck to Paycheck is A Way of Life for Majority of U.S. Workers, According to CareerBuilder Survey."
http://press.careerbuilder.com/2017-08-24-Living-Paycheck-to-Paycheck-is-a-Way-of-Life-for-Majority-of-U-S-Workers-According-to-New-CareerBuilder-Survey

We learn good habits and manners when we're young. You teach your kids to brush their teeth, right? Why? So they can prevent painful toothaches and expensive dental work. You teach them to be polite and courteous by saying "please" and "thank you." You tell them to wash their hands before they eat so they don't spread germs and stay healthy. By the time we get to be adults, good hygiene and good manners become part of our nature because they've become good habits.

How we handle finances comes from habits we develop, too. Sometimes we observe attitudes and behaviors in others we admire and respect, like I did with my parents. Of course, the flipside is true, too. Sometimes behaviors and attitudes can be cautionary tales. I've made some financial blunders and learned from them. Like most parents, I don't want my kids to repeat my mistakes, so I'll tell them about the times I could have done better with the wisdom of hindsight.

Sometimes our natural personalities can be a factor. For example, I've always been competitive, so every financial endeavor I did as a kid—from collecting cans to running a lemonade stand—benefited from me wanting to do better than other kids. I began to look for ways to be better than the competition, sought advice from my dad, and learned from my failures, which carried to more success in other ventures. You have to be willing to learn from your failures and those of others to succeed. Those can be tough lessons, but they help you do better the next time around.

My dad was a big influence in my young entrepreneurial days. He even gave me a summer job at his financial services and insurance firm when I was only twelve years old. I stuck labels on postcard marketing mailers and entered check registries in an archaic version of QuickBooks. For an entire summer. Daily.

This early work also gave me the chance to see my dad at work. I saw him build relationships with his clients, build trust, and build his business. He still is a big influence on me today as we continue to work together.

Think about who was or is your role model. What did you learn from them? What do you still learn from them? Now think about whether you are being a role model. Better yet, think about *how* you are being a role model when it comes to finances.

There's that old saying, "money makes the world go 'round." Start looking at the world around you and find ways to get your kids and grandkids interested in learning, talking, and doing things money-related. This book will help you find some ways to do that. Some strategies might be familiar to you, some may be lightbulb moments, so just keep reading.

Both parents and grandparents are major influencers for children and grandchildren when it comes to talking about money. Sometimes it may seem like we don't have a child's ear, like when we tell them to pick up after themselves or ask for a second time if they've done their homework, right? But they are listening, it turns out.

Children pay close attention to issues related to money and parents should make an effort to talk with their children, as well as provide real-world, hands-on examples about money-handling to ensure they don't develop misconceptions about money and finances, according to a study conducted in 2018.[3]

As a kid, didn't your ears perk up when someone talked about money, especially if it involved how you could get some? No kid dreams of being poor. They dream about big houses, fancy cars, nice clothes, and travel, especially to fun places they see on Instagram. You and I know it takes work to reach our dreams. We've been doing that.

---

[3] Ashley B. LeBaron, et al. Journal of Family Issues. November 14, 2018. "Practice Makes Perfect: Experiential Learning as a Method for Financial Socialization." https://journals.sagepub.com/doi/10.1177/0192513X18812917

In that same study, researchers interviewed 136 kids between the ages of eight and seventeen. What they found was that parents were talking to the kids about saving, spending, and earning, but they weren't talking about things like family finances, investments, and debt. That's where the stuff gets real, as you and I both know.

When you get right down to it, everybody talks about the importance of saving and how you earn money. It's similar to how everyone talks about eating right and staying active, but how many people actually do that? There are lots of things in life we feel we *should* practice because it's sage advice, but are we actually doing those things? Are you taking your kids for walks or bike rides? That's actually doing something to show them you buy into the idea of living healthy. You've got to do the same thing with being financially healthy.

What about when you have to actually figure out how to pay your bills, save money toward retirement, and live within your means? Those are big deals. Talking about accumulating wealth and being able to retire may seem like you're trying to get your kids to grow up too soon. But it's not. And I'm not just saying that because I work in the financial advising industry where many of our clients are working toward those goals.

The children in the study figured parents weren't always willing to talk to them about money because parents didn't want to worry them about how the family was doing, or that the parents thought they might brag or share that information with others. But maybe (and this is my personal theory) parents and adults aren't talking about those things because they don't know **how** to talk about those things. The financial landscape has gotten more cluttered and even confusing at times. With technology advancements, you don't even have to worry about carrying cash. Remember how excited you'd be when you earned a dollar or two as a kid? You'd fold it up in your wallet and later pull it out to dream about the possibilities of what you could buy. You had real money in your hand! Or remember how that money would just burn a hole in your pocket, as you were eager to get that special treat or toy you just had to have? I had my own vice when I was young: Hubba Bubba gum!

That physical act of carrying money used to be a reminder of how much money you could spend. With plastic, where no money actually changes hands, it's easy to overspend or get used to living on credit.

There are so many different financial products—some good and some bad—and so many organizations that offer them nowadays, too. Some are definite bad choices, like super high-interest payday loans that will bleed a consumer dry. Some are complex, sophisticated investment products that require a team of professionals to decipher. How do you get savvy enough to know a low credit score means a high-interest credit card that can suck you dry?

Schools aren't teaching much about finances, so as the child-rearers and influencers for younger generations, we need to do that. Maybe you've learned some tough lessons along the way or maybe you've just had what seems like a natural confidence and ability to handle your money wisely.

Handling money is a skill. It's a habit. It's not just luck or happenstance. Sure, there are stories out there about someone who says they've amassed a fortune by the grace of Lady Luck. But usually the folks who are doing well financially are those who've honed their skills and practiced good habits. Help your kids and grandkids develop those skills and habits, too.

It's not all on parents to help kids learn about money. Sometimes grandparents can be a young child's most trusted advisor.

Like me, a client of mine named Melinda started working at a young age. She called it an allowance, but she was working for her grandpa, regularly earning money. She credits him for teaching her financial values. He was her role model.

Unfortunately, too many grandparents don't see themselves as having a meaningful role in doling out financial lessons. Instead, they dole out the occasional check, cash gift, or such, but they miss out on sharing lessons on what to do with that money. I know, maybe you think your grandkids might just roll their eyes, or you figure their parents are in charge of teaching them life lessons if you share such advice. But that's likely not the case.

Unlike what many grandparents might think, their advice on money could be invaluable. According to the MassMutual blog, Susan Beacham says "[grandparents] are unconditional in their support and they have this window of opportunity to really reach their grandchildren and be heard."[4]

If you're not talking to your grandkids about money, you're missing a big opportunity to make a positive impact on your grandkids' future success. Don't underestimate the value that your stories and your influence can bring to another generation.

Melinda works in the banking industry, and many times she has seen grandparents open a savings account with an initial deposit for their grandchildren. The grandparents have opened the account with the thought that now the grandchildren will have some place for their money to grow. But that money doesn't grow. Why? Because the grandchildren aren't developing good savings habits. She expects the grandchildren aren't being taught the same lessons that earlier generations have been taught.

Melinda also has a compelling story regarding the role models that her parents were when it came to money. Melinda is the daughter of a single mother who held two jobs, so she realized the

---

[4] Shelley Gigante. MassMutual. August 9, 2018. "How to Help Your Grandchildren Handle Money."
https://blog.massmutual.com/post/grandparents-money-lessons

importance of what it meant to work to provide and save. Her father, on the other hand, couldn't wait to spend the money he earned. Melinda herself got her first paying job cleaning a convenience store at age thirteen. With the financial situation of her parents, she needed to pay for items such as clothing, and she learned early on some frugal spending habits. Designer jeans certainly had their appeal for a teenage girl, but she realized Walmart jeans carried a far less expensive price tag and were suitable for her wardrobe. With her mom as a role model, she learned to live within her means rather than spend based on her wants.

It seems as if study after study emerges about how parents' own financial habits affect their children. According to the website creditcards.com, a parent's spending habits, whether good or bad, can leave a lifelong impression on their kids. This might be a scary thing to think about your kids imitating your bad habits, so it's important to kick bad money habits and cultivate better ones if and when you can.

On the other hand, if you maintain good financial habits and teach your kids, too, think about what they will try to imitate. Your kids are watching you pay off your student loans, so maybe they will remember that when they start thinking about college. They watch you every time you pull out cash instead of a high-interest credit card. They might not fully understand what happens within that transaction at that moment, but you can be sure they've absorbed your actions nonetheless.[5] A few of the children in the various financial studies remembered money advice coming by way of stories that shared morals. One said the stories her grandmother told always seemed to have a lesson, such as not living

[5] Kelly Dilworth. Creditcards.com. February 4, 2019. "Parents Pass on Their Financial Attitudes and Beliefs about Debt to Children."
https://www.creditcards.com/credit-card-news/parents-pass-financial-attitudes-to-children.php

beyond one's means, preparing for the future, budgeting, saving, and working hard.

Use your personal stories and memories to discuss your financial choices. Remember, sometimes we learn our best lessons from dissecting a story with negative consequences. Maybe you recall not making a wise choice when it came to a purchase. Maybe you should share that story when you see a kid or grandkid going down that same path, so history doesn't repeat itself. Don't just tell them, "No, don't do that." Tell your tale about what happened to you.

I was lucky my dad was always willing to share advice and be a role model. I hope I'm being a good role model for my daughter. But sometimes what we think we do and what we actually do aren't the same thing. A 2017 survey explained that about 33 percent of kids "hadn't been taught how to get or earn money." If we think about it in this context, it's clear that parents often fail to pass along even the most basic financial skills to their kids. [6]

Financial skills and responsibility are not taught in schools and there are limited resources and organizations that provide financial literacy curricula or financial education projects to youth.

Yet, youth are constantly bombarded with the consumerist cultural environment and find themselves in situations that involve marketing messages. Nowadays, there are folks who are called influence marketers. These are people who have the ears and eyes of younger folks through mediums like YouTube and Instagram. Companies use these people who have lots of followers to market their products. It's not always obvious that these are paid endorsements. The marketing savvy of companies has moved way beyond

---

[6] Kat Saks. Jackson Charitable Foundation. June 23, 2017. "Survey Says: Set the Record Straight on Money with Kids."
https://www.jacksoncharitablefoundation.org/for-grown-ups/articles/survey-says-set-the-record-straight-on-money-with-kids.xhtml

getting a basketball megastar like Michael Jordan to hawk some shoes in TV commercials.

Companies are constantly looking for new customers, and the large numbers of youth and young adults who compose Generation Z and the millennials are in their marketing crosshairs.[7] Those generations are entering or are already in the workforce. Even for those not in the workforce, advertising companies understand youth can still be a good target because they will try to get their parents to buy products. You know all about that, I'm sure. You've heard the pleas to buy one item or another, and the various escalations and arguments that ensue, depending on how old a child is. In another chapter, we'll talk about working with your kids to set financial goals and to learn the value of buying something themselves.

We are constantly hounded through mail, the web, TV, and other means for 0 percent credit card offers or 0 percent financing for twelve months. It's these repetitive messages that can get their little hooks into you and then completely control your life. Then a person turns into a slave to that payment note or gets buried by debt. Bankruptcies, divorce, and drug and alcohol abuse can be the result of poor money management. If you're overburdened by debt, it limits your options for a better quality of life.

We prepare our kids for living on their own by teaching them all sorts of skills, from how to cook to how to do laundry. We need to make sure we prepare them for what happens when they get an income, how to save, how to budget, and how to invest. If you've learned to manage your money, why not pass on and teach those skills to your children?

Giving family financial information to our kids has to be approached on a family-by-family basis. Being in the financial services industry for nearly two decades, I have seen a variety of scenarios regarding parents sharing financial information. There have been kids who are familiar with their parents' financial situation, and I have seen parents who do not want their kids to know a thing about their personal finances.

It really depends on the ages of your children and the trust and relationships you've built with your adult children, and how well the kids get along with one another.

I have seen situations go both ways. Some kids get along great and are truly appreciative of the assets their parents have left them, and on the other hand I have seen families at odds over monies they feel they are owed or due.

You as a good financial role model can help your kids and grandkids have a healthy relationship with money; understand the value of working, saving, and investing for goals; and appreciate the importance of charity and tithing.

Look for money moments: How are you handling a purchase, a windfall, a job change, and changes in your budget or lifestyle? Take those moments and turn them into teaching moments for your kids and grandkids.

Back in the recession of 2007 through 2009, some kids may have experienced a little of how parents had to handle some belt-tightening, but they likely didn't realize why. They just knew the family vacations were cut back and things on the "wants" list were going unfulfilled.

Some people and even some experts think that, as parents, kids can be your biggest investment. They take up a lot of our time, attention, and, yup, money. So in many ways, making sure your kids go out into the world with some great financial education is protecting your investment. Whether you realize it or not, you are leaving a financial legacy through them and their financial habits.

Teaching financial habits isn't all about talking. One of the reasons I wrote this book was to share some ways you can go beyond just talking and instead "do" good financial teaching with your kids and grandkids. So, as you read, think about ways you can involve your kids in some money moments.

Who are you modeling good financial behavior for?
For me, it's my daughter, Emmi.

CHAPTER TWO

Doing the Right Thing

D oing the right thing. That can take on different meanings for different people. It really comes down to three things in my book: having personal integrity, having strong values, and acting ethically.

All of those things result not from a single action, but from a mindset or manner in which we conduct ourselves and that we should model for younger generations. I for sure learned them from my parents by seeing how they raised us, how they conducted business, and how they were involved in providing not only for the family but also for church and charity.

Part of why I'm writing this book is to get you thinking about ways to share financial lessons and experiences with your children and grandchildren that can last them a lifetime. While you need to identify those teachable money moments, remember that you're setting an example every day with your actions. You don't want to be the person who is known for "do as I say, not as I do." There's a quote flying around the internet that says, "Integrity is doing the right thing, even when no one is watching."

To really teach young kids about money, they probably need to have some money, right? Maybe you give them an allowance. Maybe they get cash gifts for birthdays and holidays. They can start learning how to spend that money responsibly. (See the chapter on how to divvy up money for saving, spending, and donating.)

A lot of kids like to find ways to make money. I was definitely one of those kids who wanted to make money. I couldn't wait to start earning some money. I started looking for ways to make money at age eight, and I've never stopped since.

Even if your kids don't turn out to be lifelong entrepreneurs and end up getting a J-O-B as a teenager or young adults, they can learn some valuable lessons setting up a business venture as a young kid, and not just lessons about money.

Did you ever have a lemonade stand or join your buddies to run a stand? Part of my journey learning about money and integrity started with the first business I ever ran: a lemonade stand. I pitched a table at the end of my parents' driveway and hung up my sign advertising LEMONADE 25 CENTS. Whew, a quarter—yeah, big bucks in my day. Then I waited. The Louisiana heat and kindness on the part of our neighbors and other passersby brought the customers (there's something about a kid sitting in the heat trying to score some quarters that tugs at folks' emotions).

As a parent looking back, man, this still instills a taste or thirst for doing your own work. At least for me it did. I thought I was quite the entrepreneur, running cash deals and not worrying about the IRS tax man. I was out there two to three times a week, usually running the stand solo. Occasionally, the kid next door would come help out for a part—a *small* part—of the pie. But, for the most time I worked a one-man—okay, one-kid—shop. But basically I had the monopoly on this business venture, until . . .

Until the kid down the street kicked off his stand. *What the heck is this crap?* I thought. *Don't steal my thunder AND potential customers—your stand is a whole ten houses before mine!*

If I had known who the "Godfather" was at that time I might have paid him a visit to see if he could send out Jonny "Calzone" Fatfingers to stop by and pay my competition a little visit. But, hey, I lived in Louisiana, not Jersey, and I was only eight years old, so any mafia scenario was out of the equation.

So, what's an eight-year-old to do? Why not do a little competitive product testing?

Let's check out the competition and see who has the better lemonade, I thought.

So me and my buddies went to check it out. Our anxious little hearts beat fast as we rolled in to stop and give it a try. What I experienced left a bitter taste in my mouth, and it wasn't from the lemonade.

The kid was charging 35 cents for a cup of lemonade, so I handed him two quarters—money I'd earned at my lemonade stand—and waited for my change. But I didn't get it.

The kid picked up his bank and another cup marked "Change" that was empty, and started shouting "No change! No change!" like the Soup Nazi character from the "Seinfeld" TV series.

What? No change? I was hot, and it wasn't from the Louisiana temperatures. It was because I'd been ripped off. I had worked for that money at my own lemonade stand and now I was being bamboozled. Frankly, this was someone doing bad business and I didn't want to be associated with someone like that. I immediately learned the pain and distrust that can happen when you're taken advantage of. I didn't want to hang around a thief and a con-artist or help out someone doing bad business. It wasn't just about my competitive nature anymore—my grade school lemonade war had become a battle of good and evil, a fight for justice. At eight, I wasn't too young to realize the importance of good and bad business practices. I'm still the same way today.

As a financial role model, you have the opportunity to show kids how to do the right thing when it comes to handling money. Maybe you'll be their business advisor when they set up a youthful entrepreneurial venture of their own, like a lemonade stand, a lawn-mowing business, or a pet-sitting service. Maybe it's when they've accompanied you while shopping and you have to point out to the cashier they forgot to ring up an item or that they gave you too much change.

Or maybe it's when you forgot to pay for an item and realized it later. Here's a scenario where the eyes of some small children were on the adults and they learned a lesson on honesty. A young mom asked her dad, the grandfather of her four kids, to pick up some cupcakes she'd ordered from the bakery department at a local grocery store. The cupcakes were for the oldest grandson's birthday party at school. Being the dutiful grandfather, he agreed and went later that day to pick up the cupcakes and delivered them to the classroom. That night, after school, the daughter asked her dad, the kids' grandfather, if everything had gone okay. She asked how much she needed to pay him back for the cupcakes. He replied, "Pay me back? I didn't pay for the cupcakes. I thought you paid for them when you ordered them."

"You stole the cupcakes for my party?" the birthday boy asked since he was listening in on the conversation. The idea that he and his classmates had eaten some "hot" cupcakes had him wide-eyed. Incredulous screams from the three younger kids thinking their grandfather was a thief erupted in the background.

Embarrassed and frustrated to say the least, the grandfather sputtered, "No, I just made a mistake. I thought your mom had paid for them, but I'll head back to the store right now and tell them what happened." He paid up, of course. It was the right thing to do.

Money matters don't happen in a vacuum. There's usually someone else involved, whether it's the bank where you open a savings account or an investment advisor you trust to help you reach your growth goals. You need to trust that financial institution or that advisor. You need to trust the people you hire when you need your car repaired. You need to know you're getting a good deal when you're bargaining with a salesperson.

I learned an early lesson in dishonesty from my so-called lemonade stand competitor. But my parents showed integrity in how they handled their money and they modeled that for me. So I followed their example.

Some businesses embrace ethical practices. Some don't. Sometimes regulations are imposed to try to protect consumers.

In 2017, the federal government set fiduciary standards for all financial advisors, not just registered investment advisors, to avoid conflicts of interest and act in the clients' best interests. Although the government fiduciary rule (The DOL Fiduciary Rule) was revoked, our firm, Evans Financial Group, still abides by that high standard: we believe that *doing the right thing is always the right thing.* A simpler approach is to call it the Mother Test: Would I recommend the same advice to my mom if she were in the same situation as each client we serve? No one wants their mother to be taken advantage of. Sometimes the right thing can be painful; it might even cost us financially, or emotionally, but at the end of the day, it is still the right thing to do. It can be embarrassing. People remember that.

Think about the cupcake story. Those grandkids will likely forever remember the time their grandfather provided some initially "stolen" cupcakes for a birthday party and laugh about it. But at the time the grandfather didn't think it was a laughing matter. He knew he had to make things right once the confusion about the payment was revealed.

By today's standards, eight-year-old me not getting fifteen cents back in change may not seem like a big deal. But it wasn't a question of how much money I was owed in change. It came down to honesty and integrity. If a person can't be honest about some small change, how can we expect them to be honest about other, bigger things?

This was probably my first lesson in adversity. I got knocked down at eight years old and then had to get back up again and drive on. Adversity can be a great teacher. It lays some truth to the adage of two steps forward, one step back. You will get knocked down; we all do. The difference is in how you choose to get back up. Sometimes things must go wrong in order for them to go right!

As a financial advisor, I'd be toast if I didn't show integrity and honesty with my clients. My clients need to be able to trust me with their money, no matter how large or small their investments, and to trust that I'll give them good advice.

Trust is a big factor in the financial planning industry. We're being asked to guide someone through some crucial decision-making processes.

I let the dust settle from that kiddo dispute. I shook it off and I moved on . . . a lot wiser, and prepared to put what I learned about integrity and the kind of business I wanted to run into action.

CHAPTER THREE

Adapting to Change

"*Adaptability is about the powerful difference between adapting to cope and adapting to win.*"

— *British writer and innovation expert Max McKeown*

S ometimes things happen and we need to adapt to circumstances. In order to do so, we sometimes need to adapt our goals. Other times, we need to seize an opportunity when we see it.

Not long after my entrepreneurial debut with the lemonade stand, I discovered another earning potential: aluminum cans. I had heard about a kid in the neighborhood who gathered and saved them from his house and neighbors and cashed them in for $8. Holy frijoles. We are talking big bucks, super-big bucks in my day (circa 1985). You might be asking, what's an eight-year-old to do with eight bucks? The Hubba Bubba chewing gum that mom refused to buy for me at the checkout counter could now be mine, every time. That pack of Topps or Donruss baseball cards, heck even two or three packs. It. Would. All. Be. Mine! That was big money for an eight-year-old. It was now game, set, match, and my mind was turned on with cashing in on a big deal.

Cans. I must have cans.

Remember how I said you need to seize opportunities? Well, I did. Our neighborhood was still in development and growing. What did that mean? That meant thirsty construction workers on-site daily, which meant a steady supply of product. It was a win-win situation. I cleaned up the littered cans around the site, and I was going to get money. I was there to pick up the cans and turn them in for change. I could almost taste the strawberry-banana flavor chewing gum, and my mouth watered. Let's do this! I vividly remember smashing them in my driveway and raking them into fifty-five-gallon bags. With that first recycling effort, I scored $17.

Kids were asking me what I was doing when I smashed the cans. So I told them. That was a big mistake. That invited competition. My second mistake was not being able to contain my excitement at my big score. Soon other kids were hanging around work sites like vultures, scanning the ground for the latest aluminum roadkill they could feast on. We were looking for cans like a kid might look for Easter eggs. We began plotting routes and game plans on how we are going to attack the work site.

Competition became fierce. Not only did it become tough pickings, but times also started to change. Plastic became popular containers in the industry for bottling sixteen and twenty ounces of beverage. My aluminum can supply was being replaced by plastic, so that revenue stream dried up.

If you have a child or grandchild that shows some entrepreneurial qualities like curiosity, confidence, and inquisitiveness, you have a chance to do more teaching and role modeling. Most employers nowadays will tell you what they are looking for isn't the "hard" or technical skills. If someone has experience or a degree, they probably have acquired those, no problem. No, it's the soft skills that can really make the difference, skills like showing up on time, communicating, having integrity, and even providing innovation within the company. It's looking for opportunities. Again, that's not always taught in schools or even in colleges. Many curricula focus on book work, reciting facts, or learning a particular trade or skill.

According to an entrepreneur.com article, innovation and change are important entrepreneurial skills for kids to learn.[7] Many companies are encouraging employees to be innovative, so even if you're not raising a future Bill Gates or Warren Buffet, your kids still need to learn how to spot opportunities and develop strategies.

Let's say you live in a neighborhood with large yards and several older neighbors. You could point this out to that twelve-year-old son or grandson.

"Wow, Mr. Smith sure has a big yard. I wonder if it's getting harder for him to always have to mow that yard. And Mrs. Jones across the street has a big yard, too. Her husband died last year, and he was the one who cut the grass. I wonder if they could use some help with that this year."

Maybe they'll pick up on where this conversation is going and figure out that you're suggesting a lawn-mowing venture. Maybe you need to be more direct: "Why don't you and I work out a deal where you use my equipment and see if you can start earning some money by asking them to be your first lawn-mowing customers?"

Help them explore hobbies and see if they can turn a hobby into an earning opportunity. If they have chores like taking care of the

---

[7] Nadia Khodja. Entrepreneur. July 27, 2017. "8 Entrepreneurial Skills Your Kid Need to Succeed in Life and Work."
https://www.entrepreneur.com/article/292400

pet and show responsibility and a caring attitude, maybe they can become a pet-sitter or walker.

Again, they may need your help in identifying those opportunities. "Hey, Suzie, you do such a great job of walking the family dog and other dogs just seem to always love you. I noticed lots of neighbors have dogs that don't get enough exercise. Have you ever heard about a dog-walking business?"

Sometimes kids may have thought about what a fun job might be but didn't realize it could be something they could actually do as a business, like dog-walking. They may find it interesting to learn that someone would pay someone else to walk their dog. They may think that a job is something you wouldn't have fun doing (especially if you've grumbled about your job, they may think jobs have lots of drawbacks, like bad bosses!).

Do they have a way of helping others understand something? Maybe they can turn that skill into tutoring. Can they sing? Maybe then can provide entertainment at weddings or other events. Again, these may be things that come naturally to them or that they have fun doing. They just might not realize these activities or skills have earning potential.

Inquisitiveness and curiosity should always be encouraged. In my case, other kids wondered what I was doing and asked questions, leading to competition. But if someone is hardworking and curious, they can manage to overcome challenges. They can adapt to win. When you nurture and help feed that curiosity in kids, remember you're helping instill characteristics that will lead to someone who has an opportunity for success, both financially and personally.

Think of all that needs to be considered when setting up your own business and help them identify those things. With an easy Google search, they research if other businesses are out there doing the same thing. They can also research average rates that someone pays for such a service. If they want to do babysitting or lawn-mowing, advise them to look for classes that teach safety and why a customer will want to know that they can safely do the job or service they offer.

I realize the ideas of babysitting, lawn-mowing, or dog-walking aren't exactly innovative, but they are getting your kids to realize opportunities and how to monetize those opportunities. Those are some of the first steps on the road to innovation.

Times change, processes change, products change. Your kids will need to be ready to adapt to change, too.

When I built my house, I remember purchasing a Samsung sixty-inch flat screen TV for our living room for $3,000. Eight years later, a fifty-inch flat screen TV was $600. The market had been affected by so many changes to make that TV more affordable. A lot of people don't understand how or why the prices of goods and services goes up and down.

Costs go up when business costs go up, like building rentals or utilities. Costs go down for lots of different reasons. For instance, with my TV example, other companies copied the technology so there was competition, supply chains got better, and production got more efficient. Of course, that means profits can shrink, too.

In the financial services industry, we have to adapt to changes too: new products, better features, added benefits. Everyone at my firm attend numerous symposiums and conferences each year because we continuously want to improve our skills, our knowledge, and the experience we give each client we serve. It's a Japanese business philosophy called "kaizen," which means continuous improvement of working and life practices. In other words, one key discipline is always working to become better.

We essentially have to be lifelong learners, but that kind of attitude often has to start in early years.

Maybe you're the parent or grandparent of adult children and grandchildren as you read this. There's still time for you to have talks about financial matters. Talk about investments. Talk about retirement plans. Talk about leaving financial legacies with good probate planning. In our line of business, we still find a lot of people who haven't gotten around to writing a will or figuring out the financial legacy they'll leave for their kids.

CHAPTER FOUR

Working Hard

I was a serial entrepreneur as a kid. When I started my next entrepreneurial venture, my dad helped me hone my skills. I made fliers with a giant headline "Don't Say Gosh til We Wash," offering car washing for $5, interior vacuuming for $2, and wheel cleaning for $1. My marketing plan was to make my way through the neighborhood, leaving fliers on the doors. I'd just circle the block passing out these fliers. Packages of Hubba Bubba gum and baseball cards would once again be in my grasp. I could buy them as I saw fit. I was getting a great feeling.

But my dad said I couldn't just leave those fliers on the door. Ugh. *This might take some effort now*, I remember thinking, an internal grumble. I had to knock. I had to talk. I had to explain my service: "Hi, I'd love to give you this flier and wash your car if the opportunity ever exists."

Fortunately, it was around 1987 or so, when people still answered the door. Especially for a kid standing on their front porch.

My "sales territory" covered a maximum round-trip distance of one mile. That was about as far as I could muster carrying a bucket with soap, rags, scrub brush, and a canister vacuum. I soon realized toting a vacuum those distances sucked, pun intended. But I did it. I had to. I had advertised it, the customer wanted it, and I had to follow through. I'd work for maybe two to three hours for each customer, earning about $7 to $10. That's a total, by the way, not an hourly wage. It was the '80s, remember.

I had to be industrious and follow through on what I said I would deliver. This was in part because, as my businesses were always neighborhood-centric, not following through would dry up any future opportunities I might have.

That helped me in my next business . . . as the Lawn Ranger. I started pushing a mower—an old-school mower where "self-propelled" meant whoever was mowing (me, in this case) propelled it themselves—when I was around age twelve. We had what seemed like two mountains in our front yard—they must have been around four to five feet above driveway level.

I still thought doing fliers and leaving them on door fronts was a good way to advertise my business. But enter Dad: he reminded me that I had to show my potential customers that I was willing to go the extra mile, that I added a personal touch by looking them in the eye and pitching my business. I had to demonstrate how I stood out from others offering a similar service. Get ready for that as you push your kids to be entrepreneurial: Sometimes advice needs to be reinforced and repeated for kids to get it.

Dad actually went with me as I made my rounds. He wasn't there to force me to knock on each door, he was there to make me accountable. I had someone looking over my shoulder to make sure I did things right. I don't need someone looking over my shoulder, physically, but staying accountable has become a standard for how I do business. Accountability is a huge factor in success. Are you accountable? Are you demonstrating accountability? According to businessman and author Stephen Covey, "Accountability breeds response-ability."

With that mowing business, I was banking $175 a week at the age of thirteen. At $175 a week, that translated into $9,000 a year. Granted the lawn business didn't go all year—it was about a good six to seven months in Louisiana, so that was about $4,200 to $5,000 depending on our seasons and weather. At the age of thirteen was killing it! I tried one employee, my best friend, but I realized I was being used and lied to, so another lesson was learned and we moved on. I did love the fact that one of the yards had a pool in the backyard and it was great to hop in and cool off for a bit before going back to work. I could do that since I wasn't punching anyone's time clock or paid by the hour (I had permission, too, so I wasn't being sneaky). I was on my time and my dime!

But I was accountable. I was accountable to my customers to get the job done that I said I would do. I was accountable to myself because I had a responsibility for my customers. I had no one to report to so I did the work on my time and my schedule, and at my pace. That allowed me to work when I wanted to, as well as play when I wanted to. But I had to show I was reliable and responsible first and foremost.

Look at that kid. The picture of honesty.

The best lessons I learned were when hard work paid off.
This photo of me with my protective goggles is its own reward.

With the money I earned, I bought something much bigger and better than baseball cards or Hubba Bubba. I got a boat!

I was on Cloud Nine when I bought that boat as a result of my hard work. Even though I couldn't drive the vehicle to tow it. My mom would drop me and a buddy off at the boat launch to Wallace Lake around seven or eight in the morning and pick us back up at that launch around four or five in the afternoon. Those were some of my best days as an early teen. Summers were spent fishing and swimming in the muddy waters, with my boat. *My* boat, that I paid for! There's a great deal of satisfaction that comes when you've been responsible enough to earn and buy something you worked and sweated for. You remember that feeling, don't you, when you bought your first car, your first house? Remember that before you dole out the cash for a major purchase for something your kids want. They'll value it more if they worked for it. Just as you likely did.

There are important chapters in life and important chapters in personal growth. It's about cultivating and harvesting a drive to go further and further. My young business ventures taught me to be better than the competition and to learn from my defeats, which carried to better success in other ventures.

One retiree—we'll call him Bill—is one of our clients at Evans Financial Group. He was an entrepreneurial kid, too, but in his case, his jobs as a kid were needed to help his family. Limited in education, his parents were hardworking, blue-collar folks, often barely getting by. Growing up in an area where coal was the primary resource for jobs and the economy, he had his first job at age ten, shoveling slag. In the summer, he mowed lawns and would pick up littered soda pop bottles from the side of roads to turn in for a 2 percent deposit. He also had a paper route, and he caddied at a local golf club. The money he earned went to his mother so she could make the house payment, pay utilities, and buy groceries for the family. This was a kid whose jobs were needed to help out the family in a serious way. When he joined the military after high school, part of his paycheck was sent back home.

His story likely isn't all that unusual for his generation, when kids often had to be a contributing source for a working family's income. Despite not getting to keep the result of his labor, Bill learned the foundational lesson of working hard. He was accountable; he had to be at work and earn money to help his family afford essential living expenses. That was a big responsibility for a young kid. He was buying food they needed, not just packs of bubble gum to while away some time blowing bubbles.

Nowadays, kids generally aren't in a situation where they have such a tremendous financial responsibility for essential needs within the family. They may be responsible for purchasing certain items they want or saving for a car or contributing to a college fund. That's okay.

It doesn't matter whether they earn money by doing chores, by being entrepreneurial, or by getting a job working at the local fast food joint, kids still need to learn to be accountable and responsible. Remember, nowadays so many employers are looking for what are called the "soft skills:" things like integrity, being able to get things done, sticking to goals, being on time.

Last, year, a study by Finder found about 86.17 percent of all parents who give their kids an allowance also expect those kids to perform a chore.[8] The allowance may not be so ill-spent, either. According to RoosterMoney, which is an app that allows kids to track their allowance and chores, shows children can save that allowance (about 42 percent saved of $471 per year). Although these stats might be inflated because technology probably aided the savings process, it's good to know kids can learn to save from an early age with the aid of that technology.[9] (We'll talk more about encouraging kids to save and offer some methods, including helpful apps and games, to use in a later chapter.)

This kind of situation can lead to entitlement, or a feeling one deserves or is owed something, to which I say: You (and your kids) are entitled to nothing, but have the capability to have everything.

One of my personal favorite quotes is from the movie *Rocky*. I love the quote so much I put it on a T-shirt.

"It ain't about how hard you can hit. It's about how hard you can get hit and keep moving forward." ~ Rocky Balboa

---

[8] Tuttle, Brad. "Monkey See, Monkey Do? Just 1% of Kids Save Any Allowance Money." Time. August 27, 2012.
http://business.time.com/2012/08/27/monkey-see-monkey-do-just-1-of-kids-save-any-allowance-money/

[9] Cison. January 8, 2019. "The Annual Kids' Allowance Report: Kids Received $471 in Allowance over 2018, and Saved 42% of It."
https://www.prnewswire.com/news-releases/the-annual-kids-allowance-report-kids-received-471-in-allowance-over-2018-and-saved-42-of-it-300774590.html

My classic Rocky-inspired T-shirt.

I have gotten knocked down plenty in business, from my first lemonade stand to today at my financial services firm. For one of my businesses, I invested tens of thousands of dollars on a product invention that went nowhere. I had success with another investment, the T-shirt above, when every major chain sporting goods store from coast to coast picked it up. A real pick-me-up was seeing multi-platinum recording artist Brad Arnold of 3 Doors Down wearing a T-shirt with my business's name.

Brad Arnold wearing my T-shirt in concert.

CHAPTER FIVE

Reaching Goals

The financial goals we have as kids are not the same as those we have as adults, of course. As a kid, I was motivated by having my own money to buy candy and sweets. Next it was baseball cards. These were typical kid-type goals back then.

By age twelve, I wanted my very own pet, something to take responsibility for. Originally, I wanted an aquarium but then my goal changed to wanting a pet bird. That summer, I worked for my dad. Remember what I was doing? That's right, sticking labels on postcard marketing mailers and entering data into a now-outdated version of QuickBooks. Now, this wasn't sun-up to sundown or nine-to-five, by any means. I was only twelve years old, and it was summer, so I was still able to be a kid, playing summertime baseball games and going to a pond on posted property that had great fishing, which sometimes got cut short when the owners showed up and ran us off. This time I was going to save for something a little more long-lasting than some chewing gum. I was going to save up for a pet.

Summer wound down and so did my duties, ending with me earning enough to buy my very own cockatiel named Sunny. I had the bird I wanted and the responsibilities that came with it. Sadly, about a year later or so, she flew out the door when I was on a fishing trip with my dad and I was heartbroken. But owning Sunny instilled a love of birds that continues today with Ringo, an Indian ringneck, and Pepper, an African gray parrot, who are both more than twenty years old now. These are some amazing creatures. Pepper has a vocabulary that must be about 500 words. She also enjoys pulling pranks, like mimicking the sound of a phone. If you answer, she laughs.

By age fourteen, I had bought my very own boat; never mind that I didn't have a vehicle to pull it or a driver's license to operate a car! I paid $2,800 for it, which was big bucks for a fourteen-year-old. The boat had a 9.9HP engine with a trolling motor and a depth finder.

Melinda, my client whom I introduced in Chapter One, has helped her teenage sons develop a goal. Like many kids, her sons want cars, so she has required each of her sons to save $1,000 and then she promised to help them with the rest of the payment. This strategy is great because it offers more than just a goal. It requires her sons to show initiative in earning the money, it's holding them responsible and accountable, and they will likely appreciate the purchase knowing they worked for it. It's hitting all the points presented so far. Being in the banking industry, she sees that when people have a goal—whether it's saving for a new car or retirement—they do a better job of putting money aside to make that goal a reality.

Reaching a goal takes discipline and action. Too often we come up with excuses about why we can't obtain something.

But it's all about mindset.

Author Robert Kiyosaki made a point in his book, *Rich Dad, Poor Dad* that has stayed with me since I read that book more than ten years ago. Instead of saying "I can't own this" or "I can't buy that" switch that mindset to "How can I own this?" or "How can I create that?" When you say, "I can't," you immediately shut your brain down to planning, strategizing, and moving forward.

Adopting a "can-do" mindset causes your brain to think and you begin to look at possible ways to make whatever that goal or dream is into a reality.

I was a musician for years and always wanted to play at this historical theater in Shreveport, Louisiana, called The Strand. I remember watching a few musical acts play there over the years and I had my mind made up that my band and I would walk out on that stage to perform, too. In 2008, I walked out onto that stage as the front man for our band, and we rocked the roof off that joint in an almost sold-out event. One of the most memorable experiences in my life was made possible because I figured out how to make it happen.

We all have distractions and things that can deter us. One of them can be the company that you or your children keep. I've had to leave some friendships behind because the person always saw negativity and gloom.

I'll go back to Chapter One here and remind you that you are influencing your children and grandchildren as a role model by how you set your goals, the kind of mindset you have, and the kind of relationships you maintain.

Another great quote I found is from an outstanding book called *The Compound Effect* by Darren Hardy: "What you have decided to tolerate is also reflected in the situations and circumstances of your life right now." What I get out of this is that only you can take charge and make those changes.

I realize I was a real go-getter of a kid. Not all kids are like that. For some parents and grandparents, it can be frustrating to see your kid have so much potential but zero focus when it comes to finances or other talents. Sometimes you have to help foster a "can-do" attitude with your kids. Start small. "Little goals are the best way to get kids moving toward big goals," said Jim Wiltens, a leadership-training instructor in the San Francisco-area schools in a *Parents* magazine article about helping kids develop perseverance. "Meeting a goal gives kids an incredible surge of energy." [10]

I know I sure felt that kind of energy and motivation when I met my goals, from buying Hubba Bubba gum to that boat to my bird.

A lot of business experts suggest using a goal-setting strategy of SMART: specific, measurable, achievable, relevant, and time-based. Now you don't have to launch into a lecture with your kids about doing this method. That would be like trying to get your kids to eat more vegetables when they don't like them. You have to get creative and include those veggies in some different ways.

"S" for Specific

For the specific, or S, part, ask your kid to tell you what they want to do with their money. It can't just be a goal to "save money." They should be able to tell you what they want to accomplish with their money and why it's important. When I was working for my dad, I knew I wanted to get a pet. This is what I wanted to accomplish. I wanted a pet because I wanted something that I would be responsible for. That's why it was important. They should also be able to be specific in how they'll earn that money—by doing extra chores, getting a part-time job, starting a business.

---

[10] PARENTSMAGAZINE. Parents. "How to Teach Kids about Perseverance and Goal-Setting."
https://www.parents.com/parenting/better-parenting/style/how-to-teach-kids-perseverance-goal-setting/

THE LEMONADE LEGACY| 39

"M" for Measurable

The goal also has to be measurable, the M part. How much would that bird cost? I needed to know how much one bird would cost so I had a dollar amount I needed to work toward. Here are some examples of questions you can ask: How will you chart your success in meeting the specific goal? Will you do it on a weekly basis or a monthly basis? Charting these measurable things on paper will help give some accountability and structure.

"A" for Achievable

The goal also has to be achievable, the A part. I didn't want a whole zoo of animals. Although I knew that would be fun, I also realized it wasn't realistic. In the end, I settled on just one bird. That's it. Don't let your kid set themselves up for failure by making an unrealistic goal.

"R" for Relevant

The goal should be relevant, the R part. My goal of getting a bird was worthwhile to me. Yes, it was a want, not a need, but it also came with responsibility. My parents were on board with me getting a pet, as long as I was responsible for it. Getting a bird for the purposes of having a fun pet, along with the responsibility that came along with it, was relevant to me.

"T" for Time-Based

The time-based part of a goal, the T in SMART, is setting a realistic time frame in which to meet the goal. I wanted to be able to purchase my bird at the end of the summer. That gave me a set amount of time to earn the money.

Goal-setting is a skill. With practice, your child or grandchild will become better smarter and more agile, more able to tackle things that require a great deal of discipline because they have experience with discipline in smaller matters.

Go for the goal! And cheer them on!

CHAPTER SIX

Divvying up the Money

Anybody who has anything to do with money needs to know how to budget. For some people, that comes easier than others. It can be a challenge to learn how to budget. It's a skill, for sure. But it's also a habit and a skill one can—and needs to—develop.

When I was a young entrepreneur pouring out those cups of lemonade, all I thought about was getting money for some bubble gum or baseball cards. What did I care about a budget as long as I had some money to spend on that? I didn't really have any bills to pay.

But as my goals and business ventures grew, I needed to get a better handle on my money. Goals force you to prioritize. Goals create accountability. Goals give you a sense of satisfaction. Goals give you peace of mind. Goals are great in that sense. But you also need to learn about budgeting to meet those goals. That's another skillset that has to be worked at and developed.

To earn enough money to keep my lawn mower business running and reach my goal of buying a boat, I used a system that my parents taught me and that I'm now teaching my oldest daughter, who has followed in my footsteps, by opening a lemonade stand.

In May 2017, after working at a friend's lemonade stand, Emmi decided it would be more profitable to be an owner than an employee. It was a lesson she arrived at through some tears. It's okay, though, this story has a happy ending, and she learned a valuable lesson.

My wife called me to tell me: "Make sure you have some dollar bills on you when you head home; our daughter is a few houses down selling lemonade with her friend."

I left my office and headed home. I got into the neighborhood and the kiddos came into sight. They were holding poster board signs: lemonade $1; the cups and jug were on the four-legged table. I heard the squeals of "Daddy, Daddy" as I pulled up. I rolled down the window and handed over eight quarters. I asked for just one glass and told them they could keep the change. Another sale. They jumped with excitement. I heard them say they had over $40.

I heard tires screaming to a halt in my head.

"Did you say $40?" I asked.

My, how times had changed. I compared their lemonade stand to my own. It was a huge success to end a day's sales with a $5 or $6 haul back in my day.

About an hour or so later, my little bambino comes home upset and crying. I go into her room to hear the story. Through the sniffles and tears, I hear, "She only gave me $15 and we made $45. Why did she get to keep so much more?"

Now, I'm not sure if the other kiddo had a reason for it, but as a dad and businessman in two separate industries, it was time to give her a little insight on business.

I looked at her and said, "Well in reality, sweetheart, she didn't take advantage of you. She paid you one-third of the gross, which is actually a really good deal."

"How is that a good deal, Daddy?" she asked.

I said, "Well, there is a cost associated with doing business. You were down at her location, using her lemonade, her cups, her sign, her table. You see, she provided everything for you. There's a cost in all of that. In reality, you got paid fairly. You got paid $15 for about two hours of lemonade selling. That's cash, no taxes, no FICA, no Social Security, no federal tax no state tax, NADA."

Ding! A light bulb comes on in my head.

"Emmi, would you like to make a lemonade stand that will beat any kid in town?"

"Heck yes, Daddy. What do we do?"

I said, "Give me a day or two to come up with an idea."

My wheels were turning at ninety miles per hour. I'm a marketer by trade and, personally, I think I'm pretty good at it.

So there we went. I decided we'd make the lemonade stand of all lemonade stands. I started online with Lowes, Hobby Lobby, and Home Depot for ideas, but it just wasn't enough. A Google search quickly yielded what I was on the hunt for: giant sixteen-inch wooden letters to make the sign of all signs.

My hunt for the most luxe LEMONADE letters was clearly fruitful.

And just like that, the project was on. We would keep it simple with two things in mind: What are you selling and how much does it cost?

Our letters arrived and off to Lowe's we went. We had yellow spray paint, a clear coat, some stakes, and it was time for some elbow grease. Grammmom (a.k.a. my mom) wanted to be involved, so off to her house we went. We painted our giant letters—not just one set, but two sets of letters. Why two sets? So both sides of traffic could easily see "LEMONADE $1." After all, I'm not new to the lemonade game.

Maybe not visible from space, our lemonade sign was
at least noticeable throughout the neighborhood.

This setup was so good, Emmi did not even want to do the stand at our house because she didn't want her competition to see it.

With the help of her business mentor (me), Emmi would embark on her lemonade stand business. She set it up at Grammom and PopPop's (my parents) house for two days. On the third day, when her friend was on vacation, she set up back home. Three stands, about five or so total hours of work, with a cup of lemonade sold at $1 a cup, brought in $78 for my seven-year-old protégé.

Yup, $78 for about five or so total hours of work. That was $15.60 an hour. This kid at seven years old made more an hour than almost half of the U.S. working population. According to Ben Zipperer's testification, about 40 percent of the nation's workforce earns less than $15 an hour.[11] Not too shabby for a lemonade stand.

She had tasted success and she wanted more. I decided she was ready for The Three Jars concept, a simple concept that can be reproduced for any entrepreneurial kid.

The Three Jars concept is one my parents taught me. It was a concept they had lived by after growing up dirt-poor in New Jersey—all the way down to having to count individual peas and kernels of corn on their plates so all siblings had an equal portion. Actually, when I did apply the concept, I first used cans from a school fundraising effort, so it really wasn't a jar. Can, jar, you get the idea.

Jar One goes for tithing, a concept important to my family and many other folks with Christian values. Jar Two goes for product expenses or the investment back into the business. Jar Three is for savings.

Jar One

As good Christians, my parents said the first jar was to provide a 10 percent tithe to the church. As a kid, I was not pleased about it. In fact, my thirteen-year-old self *hated* the idea, I'll admit. Part of that resentment probably came from the fact that there was this one kid at Sunday School in our giant, big-box Baptist church who liked to bully all the other kids. He made fun of anything about you, and he targeted me for putting some loose bills and coins in the plate.

He was a behemoth of a kid, towering over every other kid by at least a foot. When he wanted to pick on me, he would try to steal

---

[11] Ben Zipperer. Economic Policy Institute. February 7, 2019. "Gradually Raising the Minimum Wage to $15 Would be Good for Workers, Good for Businesses, and Good for the Economy."
https://www.epi.org/publication/minimum-wage-testimony-feb-2019/

my doughnut. He was successful early on, until he realized I had licked all the ones on my plate. That shut the doughnut bully down.

But tithing became a habit and now as an adult I tithe even more. Hearts and perspectives change as we become more mature, and early examples and habits play an important role in moving that maturity forward.

In my family, we believe strongly in the importance of tithing.

> Leviticus 27:30 says, "A tithe of everything from the land whether grain from the soil or fruit from the trees, belongs to the Lord; it is holy to the Lord."
>
> Proverbs 3:9-10 says, "Honor the Lord with your wealth, with your first fruits of all your crops; then your barns will be filled to over-flowing, and your vats will brim over with new wine."

Remember my client, Bill, whom I introduced in Chapter 4? He and his wife, Martha, starting tithing early in their marriage, even when they didn't have much of anything. They always set aside money for tithing. They used the envelope method of budgeting. The utility payment would go in one little envelope, rent money would go in another little envelope, the tithe for church would go in an envelope, and so forth.

Simple things like the Golden Rule and the Ten Commandments instilled at a young age can make all the matter on how our kids grow up. As any parent can attest, we all want the absolute best for our kids. My parents showed me tithing was important, and as an adult I came to appreciate that. So that's why I passed on that concept to Emmi, as well.

In Emmi's case, her first three days of sales brought in a $78 total. So the first deposit into Jar One for her was the 10 percent allocation—$8—for the church.

The Three-Jar Method is a good starting point
for teaching about budgeting and setting money priorities.

Jar Two

Since Emmi wanted to keep running her stand, she needed to invest into her business. Her business advisor (remember, that's me) suggested a 20 percent minimum—in this case, $15—would be needed to purchase the lemonade mix, sugar, and ice to keep the product and profits flowing.

If you're helping a kid with an entrepreneurial effort, make sure they understand this concept of investing into their business. They should look closely at the investment or expenditures they are making to keep the business running. Maybe they are using your equipment for their lawn-mowing business. It's okay to work out a deal where they pay you a nominal "rent" for that equipment. They also should be paying for the gas needed to operate the mower. Read on to find out how Emmi learned this concept.

Because this was her business, Emmi, of course, was involved in the purchasing of the main "fillables" for her lemonade stand. In the process, she learned a couple of valuable lessons: she needed to use her money to reinvest in the business, and that to increase her profit margin, she needed to comparison shop.

Grammom took her to the store and Emmi went for the most expensive lemonade mix on the shelf at $4.95 and handed it to Grammom. It was lesson time. My mom leaned over and said, "Now, Emmi, you have to use *your* money to buy more lemonade."

She immediately went back to the shelves, trying to find a cheaper lemonade mix. She was now price-checking, on the hunt for the best deal. Aha! She found a cheaper lemonade, cheaper by almost half, that brain of hers calculated.

"At $2.49 for this container, we could get two of these for the price of the other," she exclaimed.

When my mom called to tell me the story, I was laughing so hard I had tears rolling down my face. A very valuable and powerful lesson was learned.

When you run a business, you've got to keep an eye on your business costs to help your bottom line. If you're acting as a business advisor for that kid or grandkid, you may need to help them learn those lessons, just like my mom helped Emmi.

Jar Three

Jar Three is how I managed to buy a $2,800 boat with earnings from a summer of mowing at age fourteen. It's where you pay yourself. Remember, savings is about paying yourself, whether it's to fund a vacation or to finance retirement. Again, Emmi's business advisor sagely recommended a 20 percent savings rate, which amounted to $15 of the $78.

I couldn't have been prouder of my entrepreneur.

The cost of saving is almost a lost art. We see less and less money saved by folks and more and more debt accumulated today than ever before. Many people don't understand the concept of earning interest and paying interest and how that impacts their finances.

Americans have become horrible at saving. I found the following statistics on CreditDonkey.com.[12]

---

[12] Paul McDermott. Money&Career CheatSheet. August 25, 2017. "Scary American Saving Statistics that will Freak You Out."
https://www.cheatsheet.com/money-career/surprising-american-savings-statistics.html/

- 23 percent of American adults have less than $100 in savings.
- The average American saves only about 4.4 percent of their entire income for retirement.
- The average bank account of American adults is $4,436.
- An estimated 38 million households live paycheck-to-paycheck.
- Baby boomers (or, people age fifty-five and older) save at about a 13 percent rate, which should last them through retirement.
- Young people are doing better at saving than we might think: About 76 percent of twenty-two-year-olds have begun saving for retirement.
- 7 percent of the U.S. workforce expects to never retire.
- Only about 23 percent of American adults have a six-month emergency fund. Most financial advisors, myself included, will recommend having a fund that can cover six months of expenses. I personally use a year-minimum figure.
- For the workforce aged from thirty to fifty-nine, the 401(k) savings rate is about 7 percent.

Do these numbers scare you? Do they ring a warning bell for you? In fact, I'm deafened by the noise of those bells.

Too many people are not remembering to save first. If you live within your means, you can accomplish the creed of SAVE FIRST! Too many folks go for the opposite, pay the bills, the house, the rent, the car, and day-to-day things, and expect to save what is leftover, when in reality, nothing is left over. You must SAVE FIRST! It's a critical and crucial habit you must make for yourself and impress upon your children and grandchildren. This was ingrained into my head at an early age by both of my parents. At the time I wasn't thrilled, but it set into motion a habit for the years to come and for that I am grateful.

I'm not the only one who ascribes to this philosophy. In fact, most people in the finance industry believe that, from billionaire Warren Buffet to my banker client, Melinda, whom I've mentioned before. When you get your paycheck, you should take your savings out first, then you pay your bills. However, according to Melinda, the "Let's spend everything and, if anything's left over, we save" attitude seems to have become the more prevalent philosophy. That's the trend she sees as a banker.

When you set out on a trip, you have a destination in mind. To get there you have a map (or GPS or your phone) for directions. It's the same thing with budgeting. You have a goal in mind and you need to develop a plan. Money is the car and you're the driver. A budget helps you stay in control and not be distracted.

My client, Bill, and his family used very simple strategies to stay on their track to retirement. They tithed, and then they used the envelope system to divvy up the rest of their paychecks. And they participated fully in their employers' retirement plans, realizing that when the money was taken out before they received their paycheck, it was easier to save for retirement.

We tend to put up all kinds of barriers when it comes to looking for ways to save start saving. Let me name a few:

- I'll start saving as soon as the holidays are over (and then you don't).
- I'll put that extra raise of $0.25 an hour back into savings (and then you don't).
- I'll cut the fancy coffee from that coffee place (and then you don't).
- I would start but I can't, just yet (and you never do).
- I would . . .
- I . . .

The list can go on for days.

This is where I insert a hard reality of truth: Quit the whining and complaining and like Nike used to say, "Just do it." Remember what I said in the last chapter? It's all about mindset. I'll repeat it here and you can repeat after me: Adopting a "can-do" mindset causes your brain to think in new ways, and you will begin to look at possible ways to make whatever that goal or dream is into a reality.

So while the savings habits of millennials have been rather hit-and-miss and they've been taking on lots of debt, several reports are saying Generation Z, those born between about 1995 and 2008, are turning out to be much better savers. Some even compare their money habits to those of their great-grandparents. I am hoping this bears out because we—the collective societal we—can't really afford to have the kinds of savings habits shown by recent generations.

"Perhaps the 2008 recession slapped the frivolity out of them, because members of Gen Z tend to be more financially conservative and risk-averse, meaning they are less willing to take on major debt," wrote the CEO of a marketing services company in Forbes in mid-2018.[13]

I think it's because they were growing up when families were experiencing tighter times (during the recession that went from December 2007 through mid-2009) and needing to watch their family finances. They learned they can do without major brand names and live with less stuff. That's not all bad. As the economy has been recovering, they're probably opening their wallets some

---

[13] Bryan Pearson. Forbes. June 15, 2018. "7 Ways Gen Z Shoppers are Different from All Others—and None Include Technology
https://www.forbes.com/sites/bryanpearson/2018/06/15/7-ways-gen-z-shoppers-are-different-from-all-others-and-none-includes-technology/#e2928ed95f14

more. But if thriftiness and frugality have already gotten into their psyche, the next step should be to start putting those extra dollars into savings, into investments, and into retirement products. Remember, these are key areas where you can be helping them.

Here are some age-appropriate strategies to use with your kids to get them thinking about spending, saving, and being charitable.

For kids between the ages of five and eight, take them grocery shopping and tell them you have a certain amount to spend and need their help in keeping track so you don't overspend. Hand them the calculator (there's one right there on your smartphone) and have them start punching the numbers. Tell them why you need them to keep an eye on that tally and not overspend: because you have other things you need to pay for that month, like the house and car payments, and some things that you want to be able to afford, like a family outing. Show them how to price-check items to make decisions. Then they'll look for those discounts and savings, too, plus they'll have fun running the calculator.

Kids this age are likely getting an allowance, so start using the Three Jar method or another method that you think would help them develop good values. To help foster charity, challenge them to use their donation money to buy a nonperishable food item for a food bank or to buy a toy for a children's home. And then have them participate in giving that item to charity so they can see the impact their gesture has made. That becomes a reward of earning money too, by seeing how a gift from your blessing has impacted someone else.

Kids ages nine through twelve can start putting budgeting skills to work in various different ways. When it's back-to-school time, have them help you set the budget for needed school supplies.

Introduce the concept of needs versus wants. Thanks to peer pressure, marketing, and other factors, kids probably don't understand the true difference between a need and a want. Do they really "need" that fourth or fifth pair of expensive sneakers, or is it because they "want" to have it to show that they, too, can keep up with the Kardashians? (We talked about that influence marketing earlier happening on social media and that really plays into the kids' wants.)

Start talking about ways to save money for a goal. You can help them identify some age-appropriate ways to earn extra money and encourage their entrepreneurial ideas with sound advice. Kids this age have to be a little more creative in thinking about how to make money. Some jobs can be gateways to similar jobs with more responsibilities when they're older. A dog walker now can become a pet sitter for vacationing neighbors later. A mommy's helper, helping out a mom with several kids, can become a babysitter later. A kid can bake alongside you, making brownies or cookies to sell at a yard stand, and then become a food handler later in a restaurant. Who knows, maybe these early ventures could lead to adult career opportunities, such as becoming a veterinarian, owning a daycare, or opening a bakery.

When the door of opportunity opened for me and my little girl with her lemonade stand, it was a tremendous bonding time for me and her as well as for her and my parents (Grammom and Pop-Pop). It was also an enormous and wonderful tool that I could use in teaching her the power of becoming an entrepreneur, how to pay herself, and the importance of giving to charity, all at a young age.

Business stayed booming! Emmi's got a good start on her personal savings, thanks to her early experiences with her lemonade stand.

And as a side note for you adult readers: When you see a kid outside selling lemonade, make that stop for the sake of that kid. Spending that $1 or $2 won't kill you, and what does it do for that child? It gives them the confidence and building blocks of a foundation that they can do things themselves. It gives them ownership and responsibility. They get a small taste of creating their own little business and it lays a foundation for them to become more financially savvy.

For kids ages thirteen and older, encourage them to find a job when they're of legal age, or to start a part-time business. This is when you can bring in meatier financial concepts, like how interest works with credit cards and how interest works with investments.

They'll likely have higher-end consumer interests at this age. Ask them to do some comparison shopping, like for a cellphone, a computer, or whatever item they may be saving for.

An older teen may have their eye on a car. They may not realize the cost of the car is so much more than the price paid for it at the time of purchase, or the monthly payments. There's insurance costs and gas, too, of course. But have they thought about other maintenance costs? Things like replacement wiper blades, oil changes, a set of tires? They need to start setting aside savings that might be necessary if the car needs a major repair they hadn't counted on. This is a great time to start talking about the need for saving for emergencies that come up when you take on greater financial responsibilities.

Start talking about what more they can do for earning potential. Start talking about how college will increase their earning potential and how they can finance college. According to the National Center for Education Statistics, bachelor's-degree-holding young adults earned a median income of around $51,800 in 2019, while their peers without college degrees earned $32,800.[14] As their earning potential increases, are they also increasing their charity and tithing?

For those kids who get a job working for an employer, getting that first paycheck is exciting. But it can be an eyeopener. They might ask, "what happened to all my money?" When this happens, help them understand the difference between gross pay—what they earn before taxes and other deductions are subtracted—and net pay, which is what they actually got paid. Go line-by-line on those deductions and explain:

---

[14] National Center for Education Statistics. February 2019. "Annual Earnings of Young Adults."
https://nces.ed.gov/programs/coe/indicator_cba.asp

- Federal tax, which is based on how much you earn, how often you're paid, and your marital status.
- State tax, which most states require.
- Social Security and Medicare taxes, which sometimes shows up as FICA on your list of deductions. These are more taxes required by the U.S. government to pay for money you'll technically collect once you retire decades from now.

CHAPTER SEVEN

Understanding Credit

"**H**ey, Dad, do you have ten dollars I can borrow?"

It's a question that can come pretty easily to a kid who has an eye on a special purchase. Maybe their entrepreneurial efforts have left them a little short on getting that new game system, and they just need a little bit more to have that dream purchase in their hands.

Sometimes the answer comes easily, too: We just dig into our wallet and hand over the Hamilton. It's just $10, right?

It seems like the mantra nowadays when we want something: Just finance it. Just borrow the money.

A 2018 study by researchers at LightStream found that Generation X (ages thirty-six to fifty-one) are the most debt-ridden Americans living today. They were borrowing heavily before the financial crisis and have continued on that path.[15]

What's even scarier is that most Gen-Xers in debt don't think they'll ever be able to pay it off. Also, millennial debt isn't far

---

[15] LightStream. 2018. "2018 LightStream Debt Consolidation Survey. https://www.lightstream.com/smart-debt-consolidation

behind, with about 75 percent of all millennials (ages twenty to thirty-five) living in debt.

Not only are young Americans borrowing more, they're taking longer to pay down the credit card debt. In a 2018 survey from YPULSE, about 57 percent of all thirty- to thirty-five-year-olds have credit card debt. And that doesn't include the percentages of millennials younger than thirty, which is still anywhere from 26 to 51 percent depending on what source you use.[16]

That pattern of behavior comes at a price.

It's likely your children and grandchildren look at what you have and think they could/should have it, too. They see you go to an ATM and money comes flying out just by using a plastic card. They see you swipe a card when you make a major purchase. In their mind, it's simple to get what you want if you have a couple of plastic cards. Even Monopoly has gotten on the credit and electronic banking bandwagon, replacing its colorful paper bills with debit cards and an automatic bank deposit of $15 million for each player to start with its modern-day versions of this classic game.

We can likely all agree that credit and financing have their conveniences and benefits. Credit cards are safer and easier to use than carrying a big wad of cash. You can make a major purchase, even if you don't have all the cash on hand. You can earn rewards like airline miles, free hotel stays, and more. Those are things kids likely do not have a problem understanding.

But then there's the other side. That's where you need to tell some cautionary tales and even implement some lessons. You can't expect someone to know how to use or get credit if you don't teach them. It's like any other skill that has to be learned and acquired.

---

[16] YPULSE. June 12, 2018. "What Millennial Debt Looks Like, in Four Charts." https://www.ypulse.com/uploads/documents/What_Millennial_Debt_Looks_Like_In_4_Charts_6.12.2018.pdf.

Want to teach a kid about interest? Take advantage of the situation if they ask to borrow money. Explain that it's a loan and most loans come with interest and an expected payment plan. Tell them that you, like other lenders, have a choice to let them use your money and that you also have a choice to determine if they can use your money for free, as in a no-interest loan. If a lender does choose to let you borrow money for free, it's usually for a limited time.

Of course, don't wait until they ask for money to teach them about interest. Maybe your kid has gotten some great financial smarts from you or they've taken your lessons about saving to afford something on their own, so they aren't likely to ask to borrow money. Still, teach them about interest when it comes to dealing with credit or a loan. It's important and definitely age-appropriate for teens to understand what interest is, how it's calculated, and how it can affect other money matters.

With today's system of using credit reports to determine someone's trustworthiness, it is important that younger generations learn how to establish and use credit.

Preparing your kids to move out on their own should include conversations about credit. If you've passed on knowledge about budgeting, you should be passing on knowledge about why credit is important and how to manage it. Landlords, utility companies, employers, and insurance companies often use credit reports to see how a person manages their financial responsibility.[17]

Talking to your kids about how credit works and how to use it responsibly, and modeling good behaviors or sharing stories about bad behaviors are the first steps of helping your child understand credit.

---

[17] Federal Reserve Board. Consumer's Guide: Credit Reports and Credit Scores publication.
https://www.federalreserve.gov/creditreports/pdf/credit_reports_scores_2.pdf

Here are five things they should understand:

- Credit is essentially a loan and they are borrowing money from the company that issues the credit card.
- Credit cards charge interest, and it's important to know how that interest is accumulated and compounded. This sometimes leads to paying back lots more than they borrowed if they're not careful.
- Credit cards have spending limits, due dates, and minimum payments.
- Not meeting the payment due date has consequences.
- Paying just the minimum payment or carrying a large balance means lots more money out of their pocket in the long run.

If managed correctly, credit can be useful. But sadly, too many people are drowning in credit card debt. It can be easy to ruin credit and it's hard to reestablish.

Remember how your kids had training wheels on their bicycle before they could learn to balance the two wheels? There are some training wheels that you can use before you let them handle credit.

First, assess how they are doing with their budgeting skills. If they are spending more than they earn and keep coming to you for cash or a bailout, they are not at a place to handle or try credit. You'll be adding gasoline to a fire.

If they have a good handle on the concept of needs versus wants and are staying on top of their financial responsibilities with tithing and saving, they may be ready. Are they being responsible enough with those other lessons we've talked about in this book? Do they have a steady source of income?

This is one area where it really comes down to personal characteristics of your kids and how you view doling out responsibility. I'm just giving you some food for thought and some things to consider as you decide the best way to teach the credit concept. This can be some tricky water to wade into.

Youth can get some experience using plastic by getting a debit card attached to the checking account they likely use to deposit their income. Monitor how they do with that. Treat it like checking their homework to ensure they're understanding the financial basics.

For an older teen or anyone under the age of twenty-one, maybe it's time to move to the next step with the training wheels and have them start using credit. Yes, that's another big scary step. It's going to take a lot of trust, so it's okay to be cautious and approach this with a healthy dose of trepidation. After all, you'll likely be putting your financial well-being on the line here if you are a cosigner for a card.

There are several options available for youth, like being listed as an authorized user on one of your cards, getting a secured card, or getting a card with you as a co-signer. Whatever you choose, involve them in reviewing the interest rates and other fees and penalties. Definitely lay out the consequences and the rules you'll want to implement for when and how to use the card.

The last credit-related concept I want to cover is that of a credit score. One of the major reasons you are teaching young adults about good credit management is because it is tied to credit scores. Credit scores have become a major way for others—leasing agents, auto dealerships, insurance companies, and even employers—to determine whether one is trustworthy. We have become a number based on our habits, which is the major lesson of this book: establishing good financial habits.

A good analogy to use for young adults is that their credit score is kind of like a grade point average. A GPA is determined by the grades they get in certain subjects. In turn, that GPA is used by colleges to determine if they will accept a student or is used by a donor to determine if that student should receive a scholarship.

In the realm of credit scores, their actions in handling credit situations become the grades and the credit score is their GPA.

So here are the credit situations or "subjects" they are getting graded over, according to a Federal Reserve publication about credit and credit scores:

- How many and the type of credit accounts one has (auto loan, credit card, mortgages etc.)
- If one pays bills on time
- How much of the credit allowed is one using (i.e. the credit limit on all your cards is $10,000 total and you have used $5,000, or 50 percent, of the available credit)
- If one has had collection actions (where the money owed is turned over to debt collectors or one has had legal action to collect monies owed)
- The amount of credit one has racked up
- How long one has had credit accounts

With scores ranging from 300 to 850, the two top tiers to shoot for are around 750 to 799, which is very good, and 800 to 850, which is excellent.

Maybe you've become aware a young adult is not doing so well with their grades in certain school subjects. Well, maybe it's time to reinforce some of those early lessons regarding budgeting. Perhaps they need to be more entrepreneurial by looking for additional sources of income and more.

Remind them that just like grades, they do have opportunities to raise their credit score. First, they should see what's on their credit report at www.annualcreditreport.com. If anything is incorrect, they should take steps to correct any errors. The Federal

Trade Commission has advice on how to do that, and it's easily found online.

If they're not paying bills on time, suggest they take a second job or visit a financial advisor or free credit counseling service to learn more budgeting tips. Yes, sometimes they just need to hear from someone else that what their parents or grandparents have advised is indeed good advice. And yes, you might need to reiterate or reinforce some of those financial lessons you tried to impart earlier.

CHAPTER EIGHT

Making Investments

A h, to be young, flush with cash, and . . . wait . . . think about the future?

We've gotten to be such an instant-gratification culture that talking about long-term investments seems out of fashion. Sadly, not enough people are doing it. Sometimes it's because they are intimidated or don't know how to get started.

But needing to have money to live is a constant necessity. You'll still need it even when you're not actually earning a paycheck in your golden years. And it's better to have your money work for you than constantly having to work for money. You understand that, but do your kids and grandkids? Financial literacy and education are about more than being able to create a budget for living, balance a checking account, compare prices, get a job, or save for a major purchase. It's about reaching long-term goals and planning for the future.

If you want to ensure your kids are getting a well-rounded financial education, make sure you talk to them about investments and retirements. Study after study shows parents aren't doing this.

According to one recent study surveying youngsters and parents about money matters and their financial education, parents were doing pretty well talking about banking and basic life budget skills, at least occasionally.[18] But when it came to topics of investing and retirement, not so much. When talking about investing, 16 percent of the parents talked about it frequently and 28 percent did occasionally with teenagers. That's less than half the parents who even talked about it. When it came to financial discussions about retirement, it was worse. Only 10 percent talked about it frequently while 20 percent talked about it occasionally. That's 36 percent, or less than half.

The stats for talks on diversification among teenagers and their parents were even lower, with 5 percent talking about it frequently and 18 percent only occasionally.

As a financial advisor, I can assure you that all those things—investments, retirement savings and diversification—are important. And you likely know it too, at this stage in your life.

If you're a senior adult, you're probably getting Social Security benefits. What are the chances that's a viable option for your kids or grandkids? Some say Social Security reserves will be depleted by 2034 or so and changes need to be made, but none of us have a crystal ball to tell us what those will be and how they will impact your children and grandchildren. It's very likely, however, that they'll need to consider looking at and contributing to other investment products that will allow them to retire.

As my dad and I said in our book *Retirement at Risk*, you generally can do no wrong if you're a young investor. The sooner you start, the better off you are. It's a heck of a lot easier to start when you're young, too, because you can start with a smaller amount to invest in, rather than playing catch-up if you wait until you get much older. Those adult-age kids and grandkids may tell you that

---

[18] T. Rowe Price. March 18, 2018. 10th "Annual Parent, Kids & Money Survey," slide 19. https://www.slideshare.net/TRowePrice/t-rowe-prices-10th-annual-parents-kids-money-survey

they just have too many expenses to start saving in their twenties. They might think they won't be financially stable until they're in their thirties. That's just an excuse. Remember, we went over this before: It's about having the right mindset.

Time is precious, right? Everybody talks about making the most of the time they have. They want to make memories. People talk about quality time. Well, time is an essential ingredient in accumulating wealth. Tell those kids and grandkids they need these three things when it comes to accumulating wealth: time, money, and compound interest. When they're young, they may think they have all the time in the world. And they're right. When they're young, they have plenty of time to start accumulating money.

Here's where you can talk about the power of compound interest: When you save a little now, you'll get big rewards later. Here's an illustrative scenario from *The Balance*: You might invest $100 at 5 percent interest, which means you'd earn $5 over that first year. Now there's $105 in that account. You keep the money in the account for another year, which means that $105—rather than $100—is growing at 5 percent.[19]

Compound interest works best when you start investing early. You can work with your kids to do the math. What would happen if Emmi invested $10 of her lemonade stand fund into a bank CD? She would begin earning interest on it from a young age, and she could keep it growing for the rest of her life.

The good thing about investing young, you can tell them, is that they will benefit from dollar-cost averaging. It's a wonderful strategy that will help them because they are making regular contributions over a long time. If the market goes up, your account grows

---

[19] Justin Pritchard. The Balance. January 15, 2019. "How Compound Interest Works and How to Calculate It."
https://www.ypulse.com/uploads/documents/What_Millennial_Debt_Looks_Like_In_4_Charts_6.12.2018.pdf

in value. If the market goes down, that's also okay because the shares are cheaper, so you'll acquire a lot more of them. Then the market goes up again, and your account plumps up again because all those shares you were able to buy when the market was down are way more valuable.

Sometimes when kids see that their grandparents are retired, able to travel when they want and play golf when they feel like it, they don't understand the effort it took to get there.

Let's go back to my client Bill. He started working jobs at age ten to give money to his mom for groceries. He and his wife had a great motto on being persistent about saving: "A little eventually adds up to a lot, but you have to save the little in order to have the lot." With planning, they were eventually able to retire. At the jobs he had as an adult, he tried to participate fully in all the sponsored saving plans offered by his employers. He realized that when the money was taken out of the check before he saw it, it was easier to save. His wife, Martha, was a registered nurse. She, too, had always been in a situation where she had a 401(k) available and she's always maxed out her contributions. They didn't have a goal to become rich, but they realized they would need to have quite a bit of money to retire. They met this goal by maxing out 401(k) plans and taking advantage of other savings plans.

In this game of life, we constantly have some sort of uphill battle. This battle might take place regarding finances, or work, or marriage, you name it. Have you ever heard of a Sherpa? Sherpas in Nepal are an ethnic group known for their climbing skills, superior strength, and endurance at high altitudes. These are the people who help folks ascending and descending Mount Everest. According to *Scientific American*, 56 percent of people who died succumbed on their descent and another 17 percent died after turning back from ascending. Only 15 percent died on the way up the mountain or before leaving base camp. People train for years to prepare to climb Mount Everest, but what they don't train for is how to get back down. They get too tired, too exhausted.[20]

Retirement can fit with this analogy pretty easily: We spend all of our years preparing to get to retirement, but once we arrive, many are unsure of how to live off of those accumulated assets without running out of money. It's incredibly important to work with a qualified advisor who has a focus on how to spend your money in the retirement phase of your life because it is radically different, just like going up Mount Everest versus coming back down. When your goals and perspective shift, things are an entirely different story. You have to have enough in your gas tank to make it back down the mountain. You don't want to outlive your money.

So how do you explain investment, retirement, and diversification concepts to kids? *Time/Money* columnist Beth Kobliner wrote about some tips on how to make your kid an investing genius by making things relatable and age-appropriate.[21] The tips basically borrow from some simple concepts that we all heard growing up.

For example, let's consider the story of *"The Little Red Hen."* That story is all about investing in something and benefiting from hard work.

Don't put your eggs in one basket. That's another great truism for not taking a big bet on one thing that can crush your investment strategy if something goes awry.

Get a piece of the pie. As your kids play on a game system or livestream a show on their computer, ask them if they ever wondered how those companies that made the gaming system or the

---

[20] Lite, Jordan. "Death on Mount Everest: The perils of the descent." Scientific American. December 10, 2008.
https://blogs.scientificamerican.com/news-blog/death-on-mount-everest-the-perils-o-2008-12-10/

[21] Beth Kobliner. Money. January 13, 2017. "Making Your Kid an Investing Genius."
http://time.com/money/4616756/make-your-kid-an-investing-genius/

computer get the money to make and sell their goods. That's a great segue into a discussion about owning stocks.

When your kids or grandkids are bringing in some money with a job, you know they've started down a more serious path regarding finances. An older teen can certainly grasp the concept of compound interest and investing young.

When they get their first "real" job that offers benefits, ask if their company HR person has talked about an opportunity to invest in a 401(k). Everyone likes free money, so have a real conversation with them about whether their company is matching their contributions. Usually a company matches up to 50 percent of the maximum employee contribution, some up to 6 percent. If someone is willing to give you money, why turn it down? The other benefit of a 401(k) is that it reduces your taxes. Ka-ching. More money, more money.

Let's talk about ways younger kids can start understanding about investments and accumulating money.

Kids in middle school are quite capable of understanding the concept of stocks. As I've said before, how much you share about your financial situation will vary from family to family. You don't need to sit down with your whole stock portfolio and go over it with them, but there are other ways you can get them to understand stocks and investments: ways that they'll find fun.[22]

Why not let middle-schoolers play with virtual money? Give your child a set amount of virtual money to invest, have them choose a stock they like, and have them track the stock's performance for a thirty-day period. At the end of that period, discuss how the stock performed and talk about reasons that may have

---

[22] Tamara E. Holmes. USA Today. December 17, 2018. "Investing: How to teach kids about money and stocks."
https://www.usatoday.com/story/money/2018/12/17/investing-how-teach-kids-stocks-money/2300278002/

affected the stock. They'll likely be surprised to find out the various things that sometimes affect stock prices.

For an older teen playing with virtual money, have them start researching a company they like and its stock performance to teach them about making more educated decisions. Think about the life lessons they'll learn in that simple exercise. No real money has to be exchanged.

There are also some online games and apps that help kids with financial literacy and investing. The Stock Market Game (www.stockmarketgame.org) is a program of the SIFMA Foundation and is an interactive game you can play with your child. You'll build and manage an investment portfolio in a real-world, dynamic marketplace. It can be played by one child or as a member of a team, which makes it ideal for siblings or other family members.

Since we're on the topic of games, another favorite of mine is BusyKid (www.busykid.com). This is a chore and allowance app that's gotten lots of magazine and other press, deservedly so. As a bonus, it was created by a financial advisor. It promotes work ethic and responsibility. There are several other financial literacy apps out there, including The Game of Life, which is based on the board game, Life.[23]

Before we wrap up this chapter on investing (which just barely scratches the surface of the different investment tools out there) I want to revisit the 401(k) plan. Long-term employment, or having just one or two employers over one's lifetime, is getting less common among millennials and younger generations. The Bureau of Labor statistics reports that nowadays, a person changes jobs

[23] Marguerita M. Cheng. Kiplinger. August 2, 2018. "My 10 Best Financial Literacy Apps for Kids."
https://www.kiplinger.com/article/saving/T065-C032-S014-my-10-best-financial-literacy-apps-for-kids.html

nearly a dozen times. About 14.8 million, or 22 percent, of active and contributing defined-contribution participants will change jobs each year, according to research from the Employee Benefit Research Institute. Of those job changers, Retirement Clearinghouse reports about 41 percent of these people will cash out of their 401(k).[22]

When people change jobs, they have to make some decisions about their 401(k) with their former employer. Do they leave it in the hands of their former employer? Do they cash it out and put the money in a checking account until they find another investment option? Do they "reward" themselves and use that cash to fund a vacation? Or, do they roll it over into another retirement savings account with tax benefits, like an individual retirement account (IRA)?

You just read that cashing out is a popular option, but it shouldn't be. If someone does this and they are younger than age fifty-nine-and-one-half, not only are they penalized, but they are taxed on the money withdrawn. You won't get the full amount. The IRS requires the employer to withhold 20 percent. If you let it hang out in your checking account for more than sixty days, it's taxed as ordinary income.

Leaving your 401(k) in the hands of a former employer has drawbacks, too. You probably won't keep track of the account like you should. A 401(k) plan does have fees and charges and if you're not paying attention, so you could be spending more on those fees and charges than you should. When you're paying into the account, it's continuing to make money. When you're not, those fees and charges add up. A reasonable amount is about 1 percent.

So, what's the best option? Fortunately, the money in your 401(k) is portable. Your financial advisor can walk you through the steps of rolling those funds over to an IRA. You will want to opt for a direct rollover and the advisor can help do that to avoid any tax or penalty surprises.

CONCLUSION

Getting Professional Advice

So now that you've beefed up your knowledge of how you can be a financial role model, you're ready to pass it on. Hopefully you've gained some ideas for how to introduce some financial strategies to your children and grandchildren. Yes, you have some important life lessons to share. This book is meant to get you thinking about ways you can provide some much-needed financial literacy to a younger generation. You're capable of filling that gap by passing on life skills.

The effect of having a financially illiterate younger generation can have wide-reaching impact. What helped bring about the Great Recession? It was caused in part by people who didn't understand the terms of their mortgages and loans.[24]

People who are financially literate will be more financially savvy. They will accumulate more wealth. If they continue to

---

[24] Sara Haslem Davis. Money Inc. 2018. "How Teaching Financial Literacy in Communities Improves the Economy." https://moneyinc.com/teaching-financial-literacy-communities-improves-economy/

invest and spend money in retirement without needing to borrow, that will continue to help the economy grow. If they don't default, file for bankruptcy, or do other major financial missteps, that will help the overall economy, too. On a massive cultural scale, we want to work toward having more citizens who have more money to spend, more to invest, and more to save for retirement. Poor financial decisions can have a negative ripple effect across our entire economy.

As chairman of the Federal Reserve Board, Alan Greenspan once testified before Congress: "For an increasingly complex financial system to function effectively, widespread dissemination of timely financial and other relevant information among educated market participants is essential if they are to make the type of informed judgments that promote their own well-being and foster the most efficient allocation of capital."[25]

When someone is literate, it means they have a somewhat proficient understanding of something. If you are computer literate, it means you know how to use a computer well. It doesn't mean you know all the ins and outs of the computer, necessarily, but you can log in, send your emails, use most of the software, and follow basic instructions to learn a new computer skill or process. If you're literate, you can read and write, even if you aren't going to write a best-selling novel.

It's the same with being financially literate. One needs to have an understanding about personal finance to make effective decisions. Getting a checking account doesn't make one a financial expert. We've told you about the basics here: budgeting, saving, credit, interest, the bare minimum of investment tools. But there's a whole lot more to the financial planning landscape. Maybe your

---

[25] Federal Reserve Board document. Testimony of Chairman Alan Greenspan on financial literacy before the Committee on Banking Housing and Urban Affairs, U.S. Senate. February 5, 2002.
https://www.federalreserve.gov/boarddocs/testimony/2002/20020205/default.htm

life has gotten more complex, with kids and other responsibilities, and your financial decisions and strategies need to change. There are more involved strategies and products out there, such as annuities, trusts, insurance, legacy planning (both personal and business), and lots more.

When a person reaches that level, the level where they are moving beyond their basic financial literacy comfort zone, that's when someone should seek out a professional financial advisor.

That financial advisor should be:

- Knowledgeable
- Ethical
- Experienced
- Trustworthy
- Able to work with your best interests—not theirs—at the forefront.

To find that person, you should ask lots of questions. Tell your child or grandchild, if they're the one seeking out an advisor, to ask lots of questions. If you're going to place your trust, confidence, and life savings in someone's hands, don't you think it's a good idea to know them personally and professionally? I do. Real professionals will feel the same way. A competent, qualified professional should not take offense to an interview process.

Just like you want an experienced surgeon operating on you because it will increase your health, you also want an experienced professional operating for you financially. You want the same for your kids.

Following are some things one should inquire about in order to establish a relationship with that advisor.

- *Can you provide me with some generic samples of how you've helped people achieve their goals?* Find out if they work with clients who have similar situations to yours. That's going to be important. After all, you don't go to the dentist to have your eyes checked.

- *What are your qualifications?* Look for someone with experience and education, not just certifications. Some advisors can have a dizzying array of abbreviations or letters behind their names. If you want to decode those designations, you can go to the Financial Industry Regulatory Authority website to look them up: ww.finra.org/investors/professional-designations

- *Are you a fiduciary?* Being a fiduciary means the advisor has a fundamental obligation to act in the best interest of the client and to provide advice that is in the client's best interest. An advisor's conflicts of interest must be disclosed. Fiduciaries are never under an obligation to recommend any one product or service. They are legally obligated to recommend what is best for their clients, period. The fiduciary standard puts the advisor on the level of problem-solving, not product selling.

- *What is your investing strategy?* The answer you want to hear is that they want to first know what your goals, dreams, plans, aspirations, and values are. Yeah, it's a little bit of a trick question. It's like you getting in a taxi and asking the driver where they are headed. The driver—a.k.a. the advisor—should be asking where you are headed. One size doesn't fit all when it comes to helping clients plan for their future. Each client is unique. Each person has different risk tolerances, time frames, and goals. You need a financial plan that will fit you.

- *How do you work with your clients and how often should we have contact?* You should have at least an annual review of your financial plan to make sure you are on track to meet goals. Regularly scheduled reviews are critical because tax rules change and the economic climate changes, too. And then there are the changes that can happen in your life. You also want to know who you will be working with in subsequent visits. Will you be meeting the principal and then shuttled off to an administrator? Or is the principal going to have an active role in following through with the financial plan they developed with you? Ask about how much access you'll have with the advisor and the best way to reach them.

We've had clients come in asking for a second opinion. They already have a financial advisor they trust, and that's to be admired. A true professional won't mind you getting a second opinion. Again, you might do that health-wise when you have a major health concern, so it's okay to do that when you have a major financial concern. If you are a current client of ours and need some help figuring out how to reach out to the younger generation in your family with some financial guidance, we can help you with that, too.

So maybe you've been doing pretty well and are all set for retirement and your kids are doing well, too. You've already passed on some great money lessons and are happy to see your prodigy doing fine with their finances, too. You think you have all your financial affairs in order. But do you? Have you covered all of your estate-planning bases? Have you talked to your kids or grandkids about the money you'll be leaving them? Visit with a financial advisor and become educated, and be sure your plans are up-to-date about what will happen with your assets. It's become more common than not, it seems, to hear about some wealthy celebrity who died and left their estates in shambles: Aretha Franklin, Prince, Sonny Bono, Marilyn Monroe.

You may not be a celebrity to the world, but you're important to your family. You don't want your legacy to be one where they have financial consequences because you didn't take the time to become informed or have conversations with them. Not all assets are inherited the same and not all are taxed the same.[26]

There are various rules for IRAs; for other non-retirement tax-deferred assets, such as annuities; for stocks, bonds, and real estate. For example, the value of that piece of property is based on what it was the day you died, not what you paid for it. If you bought a home for $250,000 and it is valued at $500,000 when you die, that's the value of the asset your heirs inherited. That's called a "step-up basis." If they sell the property, capital gains tax will be calculated on that step-up basis, not your purchase price.

These may not be things you worry about working through with an eight year old or even a teenager in your family, but they are certainly things you and other adults in your family should be considering and working through with qualified professionals if you want your legacy to last beyond your lifetime.

I thank you for taking the time to read this book and for investing in your biggest investment: your kids. Parenting isn't easy; there really isn't a manual. And this book certainly isn't THE manual on financial advice. It's more like a soundbite of advice. But I hope it has helped you start thinking about the concepts introduced in this book, find ways to have money-related conversations with your children or grandchildren, and turn lemonade-stand lessons into a legacy.

---

[26] Matt Hausman. Kiplinger. January 27, 2018. "5 Things Your Kids Should Know Before They Inherit Your Money."
https://www.kiplinger.com/article/retirement/T021-C032-S014-5-things-your-kids-should-know-before-they-inherit.html

About the
Author

Colin Evans is a Managing Partner of Evans Financial Group, a full-service financial planning firm founded by his father in 1988 in Shreveport, Louisiana. Colin graduated from Louisiana State University in Shreveport in 2001 with a bachelor's degree in financial analysis and insurance. He has been in the financial services industry with his father since 2000. He is a Top of the Table member of the Million Dollar Round Table, a trade association to help insurance brokers and financial advisors establish best business practices and develop ethical and effective ways to increase client interest in financial products, specifically risk-based products like life insurance, disability, and long-term care.

Colin and his wife, Ashley, love to travel; two of their favorite destinations are Banff, Alberta, and Montego Bay, Jamaica. In his spare time, Colin teaches about firearms, shoots 1,000-plus rounds per month, goes saltwater fishing, and helps run the occasional lemonade stand. He is an NRA pistol instructor, a concealed-carry permit instructor for the state of Louisiana, and co-owns 556 Tactical LLC, a small niche firearms manufacturer.

Colin and Ashley live in Shreveport, Louisiana, with their two children, Ashton and Emerson Leigh. They are members of The Church at Red River.

The eight staff members of Evans Financial Group have combined experience of more than one hundred years in wealth management and take pride in helping those nearing or those already in retirement. Evans Financial Group's mission is to make positive, life-changing, lasting differences in the communities it serves, and its vision is to be its clients' last advisor. One of the company's frequent mottoes is "Together, let's make sure your story ends well."

Colin and his father, Dave, are the co-authors of *Retirement at Risk: Keeping Seven Predators Away from Your Nest Egg.*

Contact

If you'd like to talk about more tips for helping future generations get their start in responsible financial habits, or if you're looking to get your own financial house in order, Evans Financial Group is here. Give us a call and we'll be happy to talk and discover if we'd be a good fit for working with you or help you find someone who can:

Evans Financial Group

www.evansfinancialgroup.com

7600 Fern Ave. Building 1200

Shreveport LA 71105

Phone: 318-629-4852 | Fax: 318-629-4895

info@evansfinancial.com

Made in the USA
Columbia, SC
19 June 2021